Olive
thank you,
c

cassandra tribe

the greedy heart

mirastrar
Albuquerque

Also by Cassandra Tribe:

Angel

The House of Weddings

The Garden of Lost Things

all titles are available on iTunes, IndieRhythm.com and loveandwords.com

ISBN 978-0-615-25620-7

Mirastrar

Albuquerque, NM

USA

Content

Angel

from the cd, "Angel"

Raise your head
and look forward, Angel,
let the ash
fall from your eyes.
Stand in balance
with not a word said,
and let the constellation
of your life rise.

Too long this penitent form,
too long this grief and shame,
raise your head, Angel,
and look forward again.

The ground you need not see
for I never rescinded your wings,
and look
how the Sibyls appear
to make of your scars
such jeweled things.

I myself have come to you,
see what it is I bear,
your heart undamaged
and still so very clear.

In my years of waiting,
I have wrought for it,
links of chain
made from your learning,
so no storm will separate you again.

Let me lay your heart
upon you
and fasten the clasp.
Let the faithful come and serve you
their hands
made ready with
silk for your skin,
and oil for your hair,
drink, my Angel,
of the wine they offer
and find the memories
that we once shared.

the cruelty
of choice,
is that it always leaves us denied,
freedom lies in our awareness
that all love survives.

and even though
there is not one thing
that can be reclaimed,
within every moment
there lies the chance
to begin.

Raise your head, Angel,
and stretch out your wings.
The world has been longing
to be loved
again.

beauty mine

roots and all
her words remained
piled on the ground,
scattered among the detritus
of what has been torn down.

roots and all
tangled and limp
against her skin
petals lay still soft but
brittle they'll become.

her hungry eyes
seek mine
my silence their only view,
what we had shared
fades slowly
in the shelter of her palms.

roots and all
her desire has death become.

what fortune it was
that we met in the field
away from the house
and gardens and blooms,

what fortune it was
that the beauty
she harvested,
was not mine.

comes the wide sea

from the cd, "Angel"

and how am I to chart a course
to a place I do not know?
When these waters
beneath my hull
are full of rocks
and things unknown.
My eyes strain to see
the currents and whorls
of danger.
My ears are tuned
to the complaints of the wind

How am I to chart a course
when it is all I can do
to see the dangers before me,
and my hours are spent
making sure I do not drown?

I come from calmer seas.
Doldrums.
Drifting with float anchor,
trailing my hand in the warm wake,
the fish kissing my fingers
as we agree,

it is enough for us,
to share the sea.

I have no experience
in waters such as these.
I would not have even entered them
except for the vision of you,
my siren, my fate,
I see you and become unmoored –
my memories of calmer seas
are suddenly revealed to be
a madness that has
masqueraded as safety.

The dangers I thought all around,
now seem small,
and the stories of warning
somehow,
meant for everyone
but me.

In my calm seas,
I took my madness
to be the sum of reality.

I have no experience
in waters such as these.

How am I to navigate
when the charts I own
are not drawn complete?

How am I do this?
Me?
Who for so long
thought the absence of wind
marked a passage chosen correctly.

And you,
my siren, my fate
I see you
and wonder -
will you lead me to
the open sea,
or dash my soul
on the rocks beneath?

It does not matter.
I don't care.

For once,
in this moment,
as the winds gather
and storms threaten,
I am not hunkered below
battened hatches
waiting for it all to pass,

I am fighting sail seas of canvas
to harness the growing wind.
I watch not the surface
for danger any longer,
but the horizon
of the wide, open sea.

How am I to navigate all this,
when I know not where I go,
and for once,
I care not
to guess?

For Marthena
(who I know not)

I run the risk,
of causing offense
with this list of curiosity,
and in my defense,
I need to say it was not
your image that inspired me.

Marthena,
The Lady Goddess,
the ma'am,
standing alone on the white page
those letters sing
and lend to me with their voices
places I've never been.

Until you graced the page,
I was living in
a delicate delusion of abstinence.
Now, I find
my lips my tongue my heart and hands
caress each letter of your name
as if they were an entrance.

And there is a part of me,
yes,
that is deeply disappointed
that I know your face.

Don't get me wrong,
a nice one it is,
but when I call out 'Marthena',
it is not you
I imagine.

When I cry out 'Marthena',
The woman that I see –
is one who is equal and hopefully,
greater than me.
That could be you,
but know you - I do not.
The Marthena of my dreams
will cause me not
a question or a thought
of having said something 'wrong'
that may be someone's 'right'
and having to extricate myself
from all that riot.

You, I have,
if only in a name,
while she remains as remote as a queen.

And does it make sense?
Can you smile and bear,
that when I say your name
it is not you,
I imagine here?

Marthena,
my Lady Goddess,
the ma'am,
your name alone
brings me to places,
I've never been.

the Dark Flower of Hope

from the cd, "Angel

In my city darkness rules,
broken only
by the shattered lights of a thousand lives
that are crushed unnoticed.

Tiny points of color
red and green now yellow warning
slow, don't stop, but don't commit to go.

And we take the night
for what it used to mean
and grow disappointed
in its lack of delivery.
Our poets are silent.
Our singers drunk,
their words spilling out in clumps,
and still we expect
under cover of night,
the litter of their words will be transformed
into illuminating myths of life.

And finding them to only be
scraps of paper
wasted on our history,

we gather them like leaves
to stuff in our shoes
and pretend as if our soles
weren't holed but new.

The doors that once provided
warmth and answers
lie on streets no longer safe,
and the taverns
where we passed our youth,
are filled with people drunk
with their desire for escape.

And tossed from raucous lit life
into day just dawning,
the silence is unbearable,
making spare moments
beneath the sun,
seem more dark
than darkness has become.

And still
I choose to live here.

Walking streets
more real in memory
than what they have become
shadows find me pools
I search for reflections
of what I have known
and find none.

Turning I leave
emptiness filled with a hundred bodies disconnected
and seek the small alley
that holds but distant threat of the sun,

The key that fits the lock
that turns and opens to my
sacred space
is old and worn,
and worry do I with each day
I will come home
and it will be too bent or weak
to free the lock and leave me
trapped without
in a city
where all has become closed in.

it is here
and only here,
do I sink to my knees
and reveal to the earth
all the life I have within me,
my fingers scrabbling
to find the words I have buried
in soil safety.

In my city darkness rules,
rich and fetid
turns the earth
to deep shade roots
till they are strong.

Tiny points of color
breaking into the night
red and green now yellow blooming
unseen in this rushing life.

small breaths disturbing
the stillness of my heart,
I sit and bear the silence,
My words

unnecessary.
The songs of scattered birds
illuminating what I would have
mistaken for gloom

and I see,
stirrings of something
so slow and beautiful,
so easy to miss,
that it seems of a story
all magic and strange mysts.

but this is life
as it has risen from the soil
time and time before that I
have stepped over and past,
rushed from brick to stone,
searching for signs in the skies
never thinking to begin with the ground.

and when life and rush
brought me to my knees,
devastation I did not greet,
but the seedling flower of hope.

telling the bees

I went and told the bees my sadness
but I don't think
they listened to me.
Nothing about the way they
moved changed
when they heard my tale of woe.

I went and told the bees my sadness
but I don't think
they heard me.
So I leaned my head
closer to the hive
and whispered of my dreams.

and still, they ignored me.

I sat down beside them,
and tried to think of what I could do,
but all that came to mind
was the thing that happened last June.
When the man down the way
started to redo his roof
and found the bees

had 'combed the rafters
from north to south.

It took five tries,
with smoke and fire,
water and some things
you shouldn't really try
before the town decided
they needed to call
someone who had a real idea
of what to do.

And without a fuss,
the bees went with the man
in his funny little white hat
and odd shaped metal can.
To me it looked
like he climbed up the ladder and asked
if he could carry them down,
so quiet were they
when he removed the hive.

I thought of this
as I sat there

with the bees ignoring me.
And after a moment,
I began talking to myself.
In a quiet voice, almost a whisper
so if any one came up from behind
they wouldn't think
I had lost my mind,

I started talking to myself
about my grief and losses,
my shattered dreams,
and also all the things
that had come to be born
within me.

Good things,
strong things,
things that would see me through.
I would have gone on
but a loud droning
interrupted my song.
Looking up I saw the bees
had moved from the hive
to the branch of the tree.

and it felt right, it did,
I hadn't a single thought
to counter
what I next did.

I stood up
and reached out one hand,
broke off a piece of comb,
then turned away,
sucking on sweet honey,
I walked home -
thinking of the things
that have yet to come.

No Words

There are things I have no words for,
moments in my life,
when the voice of my heart
is stilled.
It only happens
when I need them most.

And having none,
I am left with signs
and movements,
things half understood
and their meaning left undone.

Then I stand there,
arms hanging at my sides,
feeling the heat of the sun.

the greedy heart

It would be silent
if my body did not
thunder and shake
and threaten to reveal my hiding place.

My breathing sounds too loud,
trumpets to attract the hounds,
betrayal that originates within,
and I press the palms of my hands
against the damp stone behind me
and will my body into silence.

Silence
that protects and shelters.

I listen –
and there is nothing.
No footfalls seeking me.
No stone kicked absently
revealing an approach.

I am wrapped in silence
that protects and shelters
for at least, it welcomes me

and knows that I am there.

the greedy heart that chases,
does not even really care
that it is me being chased.

It stumbles blindly
through the streets
seeking relief from its loneliness,
seeking magic
to heal the wounds it made
with its own hands.

It comes in masques and dresses
like royalty
yet remains ugly as a fetus,
all mindless want
and body demand

the greedy heart
wants without giving
gives without knowing
if their gift is burden or not
and does not really care,

such pleasure does it take
in its own decisions.

such pleasure does it take
in its own desires and wants
that it cannot understand
you're not sharing its fun.

How offended and dangerous
a greedy heart becomes
when it finally discovers,
no matter what the fantasy,
that they are still alone.

then the chase begins
through narrow streets,
before the public eye,
and in darkened corners
with great put upon cries

don't try to stop
and face the pursuit
with calmness and decency,
such things do not exist

in their vocabulary
for the greedy heart
thinks it has no right to be denied.

for if you do not want them,
they are sure,
it is only a matter of time
before you see
the error of your ways,
in this they have faith
and continue to assail
the walls of your boundaries.

Your only hope,
the only way to escape,
is to run just fast enough
to stay ahead,
find enough dark corners
in which to hide
and pray to the Gods above,
the greedy heart
will grow bored,
and set its sights
on a new bride.

in the beginning

Azuras dances,
because he cannot forget
the beginning of time,
before you or I
or any two feet
marked the soil;
Azuras danced and sang
in the loneliness
of it all,
and never
noticed us
missing.

Monster

from the cd "Angel"

Color me the black
of soil fed with death,
color me the red
of veins newly let,
color me without
shadows cast by light -
for I am the monster of forgiveness,
the demon of delight.

Even the dogs shy from me.

To them I must smell
of forgetfulness,
and as all dogs know,
to be forgotten
means to become cold.

But look how their masters welcome me,
with fatted calf and incense,
so enamored are they
with their gifts
that none, save the youngest,
notice the birds have ceased to sing.

The Elders take me by the hand,
leading me to their place of honor,
and seat me on a throne
made of children bound together.

They think I am a God,
and the only way they know
to show their love for a God
is by trying to prove
that nothing in life matters.
So they bring me wild gifts
that will grant them starvation
and give to me their children
to make of their futures
broken things.
All so they can gain from me
the forgetfulness of pain and deceit.

Even the dogs shy from me,
yet their masters cannot distinguish
a monster from a king.

Under my tunic I wear a circlet of tongues,
trophies I claim

when this seemingly
unending
parade of gifts is done.
For what use this means for speech,
when you have given up your right
in the name of peace?

simple, simple people
who think all acts of love feel good.

It is this hidden rot
that the dogs can smell,
and even they won't risk
such spoiled food.

When the gifts are done,
and distress is gone,
the people whirl before my throne,
stopping only to open their
mouths and let me lean down
and bite off their tongues.
How drunk they get on a demon's kiss,
thinking they are in the ecstasy
of being blessed.

And the night wears on.
They forget me,
gods are only remembered
as long as their need.
Save the youngest,
who leads the oldest by hand.
I see how the child blocks
the blind step
when the dance
threatens to interfere,
then finds a new path
and continues to draw near.

Such a faithful "dog" for a man
near death to have.

The old
can no longer pretend,
they see me for what I really am,
and at last
are aware of what they have done.
Blind though he may be,
his gaze penetrates
the circus around me.

"Give me back what you have damned!"
    he cries,
"For I will not die a lesser man."
    and he reaches out to touch my face.

I close my eyes as his skin finds mine.
First the tips
then with dawning wonder,
he cradles my head
and weeping,
all anger asunder,
he drops his touch
and stumbles from the room,
dragging youth after.

Had I a voice to call to him
that had not died from mis-use,
I would have kept silent
and cried tears of my own,
letting our grief mingle on the ground.

For at least he to dust
and forgetfulness can return,
while I am ever doomed

to remain on man's throne.
Powerless to turn them away
and cry warning
as they push on me
their baskets of offerings.

I am never more alone
then in the midst of this revelry,
this celebration of mankind
that is based in fallacy.

Before this makeshift throne,
they come each and their own
to lay out their tales of woe.
With a nod, with easy grace,
I give them their choice -
suffer your decision
and keep your voice;
or bliss
and the loss of your tongue.

Forgive or forgiven,
you must be sure of what is done,
and if they seek me

for lack of will to decide,
then my attention they will receive
before the evening draws nigh.

My grace has the beauty
of the bitter asp.

They know this,
but take care to remain
carefully blanketed in chosen ignorance,
unaware of the energy they expend
in fencing cemeteries in their souls
large enough to hold their morals.

Do monsters rise from the dust?
Or do we make them
with our hands?
Was I always as such?
Or was I once a man?

Why don't you ask my children,
if you can get the dogs
to stop worrying their bones,
perhaps they can tell you

whether I have finally learned,
what must be forgiven
and what must be left alone.

Bless the gods who saw fit
to so deform me
that my lack of judgment
is written on my face.

And even though I gave away
my right to everything,
they granted me eternity
to witness the greatest
failure of the human race.
And I live off their pain,
no longer mortal
but monstrous in my claims.

But, I am fair.
At the last moment,
a minor god intervened
and gave me fairness
along with my poisonous needs.
I am fair because I offer them all

the choice to live as gods,
or accept my gifts and be devoured all.

No one seems to care,
that the gifts of the gods
are not lightly shared
and no one questions
when I show up at their door
with my moment of discomfort
and gifts abundant.
They celebrate my arrival
rather than face the struggle
to reveal what of the gods
lives within,
and before long it withers and dries
never to bloom again.

Rare is the village
that with torch and mob
chases me from the gate.
In these places,
somehow they were shown,
that forgiveness is not given,
but grown.

It is not something they can
barter and trade,
it makes no man good
and brings not a magic peace.
It is not spoken with simple words
but wrung from grief,
and is not meant for every thing.

I can usually smell
these villages from afar,
for they reek of love
and calmness and faith.
Their voices are almost always
raised in song
for not one of them
has given up their tongue,
thinking it made them a better man,
and monsters,
are not tolerated there.
Monsters are not wanted,
and so I turn away,
trying to resist the urge
to look just once
on what life could have been.

I gave up my right to that,
and while the gods
may have forgiven me
there is no way of going back.

Instead,
I go on,
and will play my role of temptation
until mankind's time is done,
and then we shall all stand together
and answer
for what we allowed in our lives,
and what we learned
of the need to reconcile.

Color me the black
of soil fed with death,

color me the red
of veins newly let -

but learn to be wary should I appear,.
miss not
when the birds have stop singing

and the gathering
absence of light,

for I am
the monster of forgiveness,
and the demon
of delight.

Baucis and Philemon

Note: *In Ovid's fable, Baucis and Philemon were the only ones who showed hospitality to the Gods when they came, in disguise, to their city.*

In thanks, Zeus spared them when he destroyed the place and turned their cottage into a temple. He granted them one wish and they chose to stay together and when it came time for one of them to die, they wished that the other would die as well.

They served the Gods for hundreds of years. One day, Baucis looked up from his work in the garden and saw Philemon walking towards him in tears. He went and put his arms around her and they were transformed into two intertwining trees, one oak, and the other, linden.

Baucis

Beneath the linden tree
my love sheds tears
and I remain,
rooted beside her,
my arms two boughs,
move me do the winds,
but never do I let go.

Her grief is inside me,
her loss my own.
My words, my life
I hold silent and still
for in this moment,
in this instant,
she needs not me,
but more of herself
then she has to bear,
and I have spent a lifetime
gathering her memories and hopes,
caring for them,
storing them in feathered places
should she need to find them again.

and I shall remain
rooted beside her,
my arms two boughs,
Move me do the winds
but never do I let go.

Philemon

How does a tree know
when the seasons are about to end?

I have watched myself grow older
in the body of my beloved
though his eyes
still see me with youth.
I have watched myself
grow old and frail
and kept my tongue silent,
when he speaks to me
of the things we will do
come spring.

My love.
My life.
Whose back is bent
and gait is slow shuffle,
fingers thick
and wiry hair that grows
where there used to be muscle.

I remember your youth,
but I love your age,
for you chose to grow old
with me.

How am I tell you,
how am I to break this silence
and tell you,
that our time is at an end?

My love,
My life,
I promise you,
seeds will root in this ground
I have wetted with my tears,
and trees shall grow
that will bear our names
and they will never know
when seasons begin or end.

The wind through their leaves
will speak of our story of love
and the kindness of Gods
so the world will never forget.

My love,
My life,
hold me and comfort me,
stay with me,
twine your limbs in mine,
remain with me,
and never let me go.

what was it?

from the cd, "the garden of lost things"

Last night
I dreamed
of a city by the sea,

all the old women there
would sneak out late at night
and go swimming,

and the water was warm,
and the water was heavy,

and beneath it,
there were all these small statues
of the Virgin Mary.

The voices
of these old women
filled the night,
as they laughed and spoke among themselves

What was it
they were saying?
I couldn't make out their words
so I imagined what they said.

But why
do they only speak of it,
late at night,
in some one
else's
dream?

The Architect

In my life,
I have built whole cities from scraps of words
quilted into phrases
and baled into walls.
Knitting them strong corners
with wire from broken dreams,
I have built rooms of echoes
and forgotten thoughts.

Stacking bricks of phrases,
I imagine these things
to be architectural wonders,
when my life
would be better served
to realize,
they are only sets.

People come to live here
convinced
I have saved their history,
adorned it,
and made altars in their names.
I soften the oubliettes
hidden among my false rooms

with cushions of soiled letters
that speak of love
and end in doom
and make of these forgotten rooms
places my travelers
long to be.

To forget and remember at once.
To live in a dream
and bear no responsibility.
It's what they come here for.

With blank sheet I wander,
pencil sharp and ready
to reject all I see that is real
and transform it into
shelters of should be.

Even though,
my buildings list
on uneven foundations,
everyone walks about
with their arms extended,
to catch themselves

should they fall,
as if this state of things
were normal
and expected.

I build because
I have nothing better to do.

Do you believe that?
You shouldn't because it's a lie.

I build because
behind the gates of the east city,
the one that is locked
and no one may enter
without me -
I am building
a city of jewels
and stone foundations,
windows that stretch far into the sky,
floors that are warm,
walls that are cool
and there are no forgotten places to be.

Everything there
is crafted with skill
down to the smallest detail.

and everything out here,
all my paper walls and leaning roofs,
has been remade but with skill there.

Made to last until the end of time.

And people live there,
yes they do,
I seem to be the only one
interested in stepping outside.
People live there,
anyone can move in,
all you have to do,
is realize the extent of
these paper lies and begin to desire
permanent things.

then I will open the gates
to the jeweled city
and carry you in.

The Wicker Heart

Why is it,
when all at last falls silent
and the World turns to me
to listen to my song,
I have nothing to sing?

No words, or thoughts,
images or harmony.

I stand there,
with my mouth hanging open,
my tongue beginning to dry,
looking back at the World with
unblinking eyes
as it looks at me,
until the World sighs,
and turns away
to more lively things.

Leaving me stunned,
and filled with an ache,
that becomes a pain,
that rises and then roars
through my chest

into my throat
threatening to become tears,
but it is words instead,
that tumble over my walls
and pile at my feet.

Only too late,
words must be listened to,
or they grow dead.

And like an old man,
I sweep
the leaves of my self
off the porch of my soul
like so much unwelcome clutter.

Their colors still
so beautiful and promising,
yet so fragile,
they crumble
and become
little more than dust,
that marks the passage of feet.

the tree behind me

It's been forever now,
since I have been
where I am from.

I've visited all the places I have known
the lakes and creek and roads,
slept in the houses
that held my youth and dreams,

but it's been forever now,
since I have been
where I am from.

I wonder, sometimes,
if it still exists on a map.

A small solid place
that inside,
seemed as large as the world.
The walls thick and proof
against sound and cold,
the fire in the grate
making the air smell
like a holiday.

And company,
there always was,
whether I knew them well or not,
liked them some or a lot.
One had only to turn the corner,
or climb the stair,
to find that there was
some one else there.

I'm not sure
what happened to all that.
You see,
one day in the midst
of the same as all,
there came a storm -
nothing grand of godlike,
just a summer storm
with refreshing wind,
just strong enough
to fell the tree
that had grown
outside the window
where it could always be seen.

I can't help but think,
if someone had spoken to me
in that moment,
if a guest had come down the stairs
wondering how to make the water hot,
I would have only thought
for a moment
what was no thought
and then pushed it aside,
but uninterrupted,
that thought took my hand
and led me outside.

To see the tree
I had always known
and seen in my dreams,
taller than it was in the day,
lying tilted
and pulled from the ground.

I didn't look inside and suddenly discover
that all I thought green and alive,
was not.

I didn't look in the hole
where the roots had been
and discover a cavern of secrets,
I did not.

I didn't do any of those things.

I went outside
and looked
at the tree I had always known
and saw it tilted and pulled from the ground.
I could see the sap running from the
heart to the scars,
and I thought that thought
that was no thought at all.

And that thought
took me by the hand
and we started to walk.

Through the fields and into the forest
I had always found so frightening
I walked,
until when I turned around,

the place where I had been,
was hidden
by the tree
behind me.

Now today,
I have few friends,
and even less moments
of just company.
But I find,
despite a few moments of longing,
that seem to come
in the heat of the day,
I have my fill
more then I have known before.

But it can change,
the way life is wont to change
in a second or so,
when you think
you would have been better off
interrupted
and turned from that window.

yet had I been,
I realize now,
although it has taken me years,
had I been,
I would not
have found myself
here, at all.

now that I am undone

Now that I am undone,
I can speak as if I was alone
and have no worry or fear
that I could hurt you
or be the cause of your tears.

Disappoint you with my reality,
frighten you with proximity,
or worst of all,
admit to us both,
the extent of my
vulnerability.

But now that I am undone,
with tears paused
and grief for a moment gone,
I can sit on the bed
rocking slowly
and take my words from hiding,
cleaning off the dust that
has gathered there,
and let them light up this room.

I am in love with you.

And with each passing moment,
each new thing learned,
this love becomes larger
as does my awareness
that I have no idea what it means.
There are some moments,
when I doubt,
I am even capable of such a thing.

It's like –
walking into a room that is filled
with a vast amount of air
so rich in oxygen,
yet sometimes so full of despair.

I was supposed
to be smarter than this,
and wait at the gate
for convenience and timing's sake.
Not wander off
after beautiful birds
past the gate and over the lawn
into the garden and up the oak tree
where I found their nest,

and became undone.
All my carefully built walls
came tumbling down
and I was not prepared for this.

When I raced from the garden,
up to your room,
to share with you my discovery,
I found you only half dressed.
Not ready for anything,
let alone a common bird's nest.

You were not ready for me
to be anywhere but waiting at the gate,
for your convenience and timing's sake.

and do you know?
It wasn't until I returned to my room,
and sat on the bed,
rocking back and forth
and holding my head,
that I began to cry
and in crying was finally free

to realize that I loved you,
and you were
unavailable to love me.

Now that I am undone,
I can speak as if
I were alone.
And what I say to myself
is a promise and a gift,
to never again
try to stand so still,
that it is as if
I have ceased to exist.

the dreams of bees

from the cd, "Angel"

Is this then,
what love is?

A strong cold fire
that burns through my soul
reducing to ash
the things I have used
to build my walls?

I have searched and searched.
I have been
to books
and fires
and circles
and roads
and at least I learned,
or so I thought,
that love begins
far above us all.

I thought that,
the worship of things
we can never know,
the rituals and romance,

would bring with it
reward
that I could hold.

So I set about
to build a life
that begged for the right
to be happy and whole.

And I turned and searched
through every part
of my soul
to try and make it
clean and perfect.

So that,
when I bent my head and prayed,
someone else would decide
that I deserved
for all that I cried.

And the gods,
laughed,
and made fun

of my small attempts
to worship them.

For what were my offerings,
my sacrifices,
my words and prayers,
when offered to the ones
who had created those very things?

What use is it to offer to a God
that which they made?

And what was I really offering?
I was so lost and bleeding
in the puzzle of my own world,
wanting God to fix things
that I hadn't a thought as
to what a God might need.

God does not want songs,
and prayers,
and incense,
and pretty things.
God doesn't want

my complaints and needs
all in a few minutes of my day

God wants everything.

And so,
the gods laughed at me.

In my robes and beads
trying so hard
to ignore
what they were trying
to give to me.

I was like the woman
who hides in the dark
in a city made of light,
clinging to a twisted
image of a god in death
when all around me,
on every street corner,
for anyone to see,
there were statues of a God
laughing and free of pity.

And the people would come out
and pour water over the stone
when the heat had grown
and threatened to burn the day.

That was the god of life and love.
That was a life of worship.
For they asked not
of the God
but took care of it.

And I watched them,
from the dank coolness
of my moss covered grave.

I watched them,
and wondered why it was
I never had a cause
to celebrate.

My god,
my lord,
my savior,
my saint,

how long would you have left me
there in that tomb?

How long would you have left me?

And I am angry,
although I understand,
that it is not for a God
to reach out a hand.

I started with the means
to be
and it is my own fault,
my own fault,
if I have chosen
not to be free.

But,
I choose it now.

I choose it.
I demand it.
I deserve it.

And look,
this is what happened.

For the first time,
I did not
bow my head and kneel.
I threw myself down on the ground
knocking aside the bells and candles,
crushing all those pretty words.

For the first time,
I threw myself down on the ground.
I rent my clothes in two.
I pounded the earth
and shook my fist at the sky
and I demanded
of the things
I have no name
that I be given
the life
of which I dream.

And look,
what happened.

You appeared,
from out of nowhere,
with no guile
or guise,
or reasoned desire
on my part,
trying to talk myself into believing
that you were something
that you were not.

As I have done
before,
time and time again.

Neither of us were looking,
yet both of us had received,
invitations
to a feast.

Yet instead of food,
instead of wine,
I have filled my cup with you,
and ever so slowly,
I drink.

But you pour over the rim
laughing to think
I would try to sip
that which must be consumed
drowning the pulse of my heart
with the flood
of my need for you.

Drowning me,
flooding the well of my being
and lifting my soul
on the tide of your joy
higher
and higher
shattering my mind
and setting it free.

It is crying,
I love you,
when all reason
deems,
there can be no way,
no how,
too soon.

But,
I do.

I love you.

And I will always love you,
because I have loved you
before you came.

And even if you left again,
this love
would be what remained.

You,
are a part of something
so much larger,

a gift,
a blessing,
an answer.

How can I deny you,
when you are what I dreamed?
How can I deny you

when my body
thunders your name?

And I feel,
I feel the smile of the Gods above,
as for once,
for once,
they see me accept
a gift they have given.

For once,
they have spoken,
and I have listened.

And life changes,
I know life changes
and nothing remains the same.

Forever sometimes
may only mean
a year and a day.

Yet right now,
right now,

I say and believe,
that I would do anything
to keep you with me.

Yet I know,
the moment I try to catch this,
to capture it
and hold it,
is the moment it goes away.

Life exists
not in our memories,
our safety
and security,
but in the ever changing moments
of the day to day.

Forever is built
not on a promise,
not on words,
but on moments –
seconds.

And God above,
let me
have this dream.

So human.
So small.

Just for now,
let me dream
the dreams of forever.

Let me drink and be full,
of something
that is
so -
beautiful.

life in pieces

Why do we brush against
the lives we should be living?
Why do we tell our children
we are all the same?
What has happened to genius,
and saints and talent?
What has become of the competent man?

What is it worth?
What have you decided?
Why do you live your life in pieces,
rather than seek to be whole again?

In the city there is a man
who holds up the world with just one hand,
and when he lets go,
when he lets go,
the earth still turns
and he is free again.

Here are the things I know to be true -
nothing you don't have
is worth getting,

the only things of value
are those you have earned.
Heaven and hell lie within you
and the perfect life ,
roots in the soil
of the one you have known.

Love is more precious than anything
and the thing we least understand.
People are not
a food to fill us,
and our thoughts and secrets
and interior lives
are what makes a pauper -
a rich man.

Why do we live our lives
in pieces,
when it is truly
all we hold in our hands?
All it would take
is a little attention,
and what was broken,
would be whole again.

The Map of Your Heart

God knows

what lies in my soul

when I stand before you

He silences

my tongue and says

"Your reasons are enough for me."

Cassandra Tribe holds a BFA from the Rhode Island School of Design, did her studies for her M.Div at the American Christian College and Seminary, and studied sociology at the Stratford. In between, she has served in the 8th U.S. Army as Military Police and traveled extensively in her former career as an ironworker. She currently makes her living as a fulltime freelance writer and editor and travels the world teaching and performing.

She is considered one of the top performance poets of all time and her cd, Angel, has received numerous awards including the 2008 Grindie for best spoken word recording.

You can find out more about her work on the website, loveandwords.com.

All of her recordings are available on 'iTunes' and Amazon.com. Her daily blog can be found on her website, myspace and in numerous other locations. Cassandra Tribe may also be followed on Twitter (caribe).

You can contact Cassandra Tribe via email:
info@loveandwords.com

or on myspace at:
myspace.com/love_and_words

www.ingramcontent.com/pod-product-compliance
Lightning Source LLC
LaVergne TN
LVHW091008080826
845145LV00003B/1173

* 9 7 8 0 6 1 5 2 5 6 2 0 7 *